Incredible People

KEVIN McFARLAND

Illustrated by
LUIS DOMINGUEZ

Hart Publishing Company New York City

Alphabetical Contents

The girl with one eye

In 1793, the Clément family of Tourcoing, France, was stunned at the sight of their new child, a daughter. The girl was born with one eye in the center of her forehead.

She was indeed a replica of the giant Cyclops of Homer's *Odyssey*. Otherwise normal, the girl lived until the age of 15.

Tamerlane built pyramids
from the skulls of his victims

In 1336, an obscure tribal chieftain, living near the Central Asian city of Samarkand, celebrated the birth of a son. The Mongol chieftain named his baby Timur. Later, when Timur was crippled by an arrow, he received his nickname, Timur-i-Leng, or Timur the Lame. To the Western world, he is more familiar as Tamerlane.

Making Samarkand his capital, Tamerlane set out on a decades-long campaign to subjugate the world to his rule. He created an empire that stretched from the Ganges River in India to the very gates of Europe. Much of present-day Russia, including Moscow, was incorporated into his domains.

Merciless to his enemies, Tamerlane ravaged huge areas, reduced great cities to rubble, and slaughtered hundreds of thousands. Indeed, he left cruel testimonials to his victories by building great pyramids from the skulls of his victims— 70,000 at Isfahan, 90,000 in Baghdad, and 100,000 at Delhi. At Sebsewar in Persia, the merciless monarch enclosed 2,000 live people inside a brick and mortar tomb.

The woman who gave birth to 69 children

Actually, there are two such women: Mrs. Fyodor Vassilet of Russia and Mrs. Bernard Scheinberg of Austria.

Mrs. Vassilet achieved her prodigious total of 69 in 27 confinements. She gave birth to four sets of quadruplets, seven sets of triplets, and 16 pairs of twins. If you add up these figures, you'll see that not one confinement produced a single birth. Mrs. Vassilet enjoyed considerable renown, and appeared at the court of Czar Alexander II. She died in 1872.

Mrs. Scheinberg's story is remarkably similar to that of Mrs. Vassilet. She, too, gave birth in 27 confinements; none of these produced less than two children; and miraculously, she likewise gave birth to four sets of quadruplets, seven sets of triplets, and 16 pairs of twins!

When Mrs. Scheinberg died at the age of 56 in 1911, her husband Bernard remarried, and had 18 children by his second wife. Bernard Scheinberg had sired a grand total of 87 progeny.

The man in the "iron" mask

In 17th-century France, when Louis XIV proclaimed, *"L'état c'est moi!"*—"I am the State!"—the glutted prisons were France's busiest institutions. Louis could ruin a life with a carefree flourish of the royal quill. But though the "Sun King" chose his victims indiscriminately, there were at least *apparent* reasons why a poor wretch might have incurred the King's displeasure.

But not so for The Man in the Mask. Why he lingered "in durance vile" no one knew. No one knew *then*—no one knows *now*!

In 1669, a tall, well-dressed man of courtly bearing was turned over to Monsieur Saint-Mars, Governor of the fortress of Piguerol. Monsieur Saint-Mars treated his prisoner with great respect, permitting him such privileges as books and the comfort of a priest. But there was one thing Monsieur Saint-Mars would *not* allow: the prisoner was never permitted to show his face. For 34 long years, the prisoner wore a mask of black velvet—wore it because to take it off meant death; wore it, perhaps, to hide a face whose agony might shame the King.

Alexander Dumas romanticized this story in his great novel *The Man in the Iron Mask*. But it is a

well-authenticated fact that the mask was fastened to the prisoner's face not by rivets of steel, but by rivets of fear.

Why did Louis XIV condemn this man to a

living death? Why did he go to such extremes to hide this man's identity? Why did he spare the man at all? These are questions which historians, after centuries of research, have been powerless to answer.

Some have suggested that the prisoner was an illegitimate son of Louis XIV, and was jailed because he represented a threat to his half-brother, the Dauphin, heir to the throne.

Others maintain that the prisoner was Eustache d'Auger, a young participant in the Black Masses conducted by the notorious prisoner, Madame de Brinvilliers. Supposedly, one of the several participating ladies who later became royal mistresses saved d'Auger from the guillotine by begging mercy from Louis XIV.

Still another view is that the prisoner was a twin brother of Louis XIV, imprisoned to avoid a contest for the throne. Because of his royal blood, he was treated with the dignity due his station. His face was covered to avoid identification.

Intriguing possibilities, all—but whether any of these postulations are true, no one can say with certainty.

Robert Earl Hughes, the fattest man who ever lived

In 1926, a bouncing 11½-pound boy was born into the Hughes family of Fish Hook, Illinois. Christened Robert Earl, this Hughes boy was obviously meant for big things. At the age of six, he tipped the scales at 203 pounds; four years later, he weighed 378. He didn't stop adding avoirdupois until he had nearly tripled that weight.

In the last year of his life, spent with a touring carnival, Hughes had his dimensions reliably measured. His weight was 1,069 pounds; his waist was 124 inches around, exceeding the measure of his chest by two inches.

In July of 1958, Hughes came down with a case of measles. Though Hughes was gravely ill, he

could not enter the hospital in Bremen, Indiana, where the carnival had stopped, for he could not pass through its door. Hughes' specially built house trailer was kept in the hospital parking lot, where oxygen could be administered and doctors and nurses could check on him.

All this attention proved to no avail. The measles cleared up, but were immediately followed by uremia—a failure of the kidneys. Robert Earl Hughes passed away on July 10, 1958. His coffin, as large as a piano case, was transported to a cemetery in Mount Sterling, Illinois, via a moving van. The weight of the coffin plus its occupant was over a ton; Hughes had to be lowered into the earth by a crane.

There is another American who is reputed to have weighed more than Hughes. Johnny Alee of Carbon, North Carolina (1858-1887), allegedly tipped the scales at 1,132 pounds. However, no reliable verification of this figure exists.

Others were reported to have weighed more than Robert Earl Hughes, but not only is this unverified, but these obese men lost considerable weight and lived as mere 400-to-500-pounders.

Menuhin was a great violinist at 11

When Yehudi Menuhin was 11 years old, he was hailed by many music experts as the most gifted natural violinist ever to have appeared on the concert stage. Wearing shorts and an open shirt, he performed Beethoven's "Violin Concerto," accompanied by the New York Philharmonic Orchestra. His technical virtuosity and musical insight were such that both critics and public could hardly believe their ears. Even members of the orchestra wept.

The son of a chicken farmer and a schoolteacher, Menuhin achieved world fame with a minimum of musical training. In fact, his violin instructors were so overwhelmed by the effortless purity of his playing that they hesitated to meddle with his style at all. Menuhin played classical compositions at the age of four, and made his stage debut with the San Francisco Symphony Orchestra at seven.

Now over 65, Menuhin remains one of the world's greatest violinists. Unlike many prodigies, he has grown up to be both a happy and successful adult.

The Cherry Sisters' terrible acting made them famous and rich

Perhaps the strangest success story in the theatrical world is that of the fabulous Cherry Sisters. Leaving their home in the Iowa corn country in 1893, the four girls made their debut in Cedar Rapids in a skit they wrote themselves. For

three years, the Cherry Sisters performed to packed theaters throughout the Middle West; people came to see them just to find out if they really were *that* bad. Their unbelievably atrocious acting enraged critics and provoked spectators to throw vegetables at the "actresses." Wisely, the sisters thought to travel with an iron screen which they could erect on stage for self-defense.

By 1896, the girls were offered a thousand dollars a week to perform on Broadway.

Seven years later, after the Cherry Sisters had earned the then respectable fortune of $200,000, they retired from theatrical life for the more peaceful life down on the farm. Oddly enough, these successful Broadway "stars" remained convinced to the end that they were truly the most talented actresses to grace the American stage.

Theresa Vaughn had 62 husbands—at age 24

On December 19, 1922, Mrs. Theresa Vaughn was brought up before the Police Court of Sheffield, England. The 24-year-old woman had remarried without obtaining a divorce from the dissatisfied Mr. Vaughn.

It was not until the hearing, however, that the police learned of the scope of the woman's bigamy. A contrite Mrs. Vaughn confessed that since she and her first husband had parted ways five years earlier, she had married 61 men. Traveling widely through the British Isles, Germany, and South Africa, Theresa had accumulated husbands at a rate of better than one a month!

Sharon Adams sailed alone across the Pacific

On July 26, 1969, Sharon Sites Adams, a 39-year-old California homemaker, sailed her thirty-one-foot ketch into San Diego harbor.

She was given a warm, emotional welcome by her husband, a professional sailing instructor, and by hundreds of enthusiastic friends, relatives, and admirers.

Sharon Adams had just become the first woman ever to sail alone across the Pacific Ocean. She had covered the 5,618-mile distance from her starting point, Yokohama, Japan, to San Diego, in 74 days, 17 hours, 15 minutes.

It was on October 8, 1918 that a small group of American soldiers were surrounded by Germans in the Argonne Forest of France. On all sides were German machine-gun nests. The wounded sergeant of the troop, unable to continue, passed command to a young corporal named Alvin York. Capture seemed imminent. But the boy from

Alvin York captured 130 German prisoners

Fentress County, Tennessee did not give up. Instead he stood up and, flattening his body against a tree, began to fire. Twelve Germans fell in short order. In stark amazement and fury, eight Germans charged down a hill at the lone American soldier. York fired eight times and slew all eight. The other Germans, not knowing that they had surrounded a handful of American soldiers, thought that they *themselves* were outmanned. They abandoned their positions to surrender.

Soon York discovered that he had captured 92 *prisoners*. The six Americans under York's command were really in a spot: they were in German territory, and they were vastly outnumbered by their prisoners. But again young York was equal to the task. He marched the prisoners ahead of him, toward the American lines. Whenever they came to another machine-gun nest, the gunners assumed that a large army battalion was behind the group of prisoners walking toward them. By the time York reached the American lines, he had collected 132 prisoners and had put out of action 13 machine-gun nests. He later received the highest governmental awards from the U.S. and France.

Edward Mordrake, the modern-day Janus

The Roman god Janus, custodian of the universe, was generally portrayed with two faces, one in front and one in back. This image symbolized the god's watchfulness, his ability to see all.

Only one mortal has ever shared this trait with Janus—the unfortunate Edward Mordrake. Born into an aristocratic English family, Edward had a face on the back of his head in addition to the face on the front. As he walked toward you, young Edward presented a genial visage. But if you chanced to look back at him after he passed you, Edward seemed a monster. His rear face had eyes, lips, nose, and ears, but the only expression it ever manifested was a mad leer. While Mordrake could see through his back eyes, the mouth was incapable of speech or eating.

Unlike the Roman Janus, whose two faces were identical, Edward Mordrake's head was the battleground between a Jekyll and a Hyde. And as in the Stevenson tale, the Hyde half won out: Mordrake died in an insane asylum.

John Popham, a robber, became Chief Justice of England

When Sir John Popham was a law student in London, he led a wild and spendthrift life. In need of money and in search of adventure, young Popham armed himself with pistols and ventured out into the city after dark to rob the passersby.

Later on, during the reign of Queen Elizabeth I, this same John Popham rose to the highest post in the English judiciary. He became Chief Justice of England in 1592, and held that high office until his death in 1607.

The secret of Stradivarius

Antonius Stradivarius was born in 1644. Initially a woodcarver, he learned to play the violin and consequently became interested in the making of violins. At eighteen he became an apprentice to Niccolo Amati, the famous violinmaker of Cremona.

In 1680, he left Amati's shop and began to work for himself. He experimented with his violins, giving them many different shapes. He was obsessed with the desire to make his violin sound as lovely as a beautiful human voice. He decorated his violins so exquisitely—inlaying them with mother of pearl and ivory and ebony—that not only are they the world's most wonderful violins because of their exquisite tone, but they are also the most beautiful violins ever created.

By the time he was 40 years old, he was a renowned and extremely wealthy man. He kept his notes safely locked up. Not even his two sons, who labored with him in his workshop, knew his secrets. During his long life of 94 years, he made at least 1,116 instruments.

The hunt for the secret of Stradivarius has been carried on ever since his death in 1737. His violins have been carefully measured and copied in every

detail, and some very fine violins have been made; but they have never attained the perfection of the master's instruments. Vuillane, a famous French violinmaker of the early 1800's, spent all his life searching for the secrets of the great Stradivarius. At last, he finally got in touch with Giacomo Stradivarius, the great grandson of the master. Giacomo told Vuillane that he had discovered in an old family Bible a formula for varnish which he believed to have been Antonius Stradivarius' own special formula. Giacomo said he had told no one about it and, even though he was sorely tempted during financial straits to sell it, he had made the decision that he would give nobody the priceless prescription except a member of the family, should any one of them decide to pursue the trade of violinmaker.

Diverse suppositions have been made about what makes the violins of Stradivarius supreme. Some have attributed the characteristic sound of his violins to the physical properties of the wood, or to the shape of the instruments; others maintain that the secret lay in the interrelation of the various parts of the instruments. Still others see the answer as the special pitch which Stradivarius derived from the sap of trees then growing in Italy which have since disappeared. No one has been able to discover his secret. It is as much a mystery today as it was nearly 250 years ago.

Fakir Agastiya held his arm upraised for 10 years

In 1902, Fakir Agastiya of Bengal, India, raised one arm straight above his head. Agastiya was a Hindu for whom all pleasures and pains of the body are *maya*—illusion. Agastiya adopted his peculiar—to Western minds—stance, out of religious conviction.

For the first three months after assuming such a position, one experiences excruciating pain, unless he is truly a master of mind over matter. After three months, however, keeping one's arm upraised is a comparative breeze; by that time, the limb is absolutely rigid, with little or no blood circulation.

Agastiya's arm was utterly without function except for the palm, where a bird built its nest. His shoulder joint was locked, so that even if Agastiya had desired to lower his arm, he could not have done so.

Not even the fakir's death in 1912 would bring that arm to rest at his side. When Agastiya was laid to rest, it was with arm upraised and with palm open.

Thomas Stevens rode around the world on a high-wheeled bicycle

In the 1880's, the bicycle consisted of an enormously high wheel in the front and a minuscule wheel in the rear. It was hard enough to handle on paved roads, and practically impossible to ride on the rough roads in the country. But Thomas Stevens vowed that he would pedal his way around the world.

Stevens was up against a few obstacles from the very start. For one thing, he didn't know how to ride a bike. But a little matter like that didn't seem to bother him. After just a few days of practice, Tom was off.

He left San Francisco in April, 1884. In August, having pedaled over more than 3,000 miles of rough roads and trails, he reached Boston. There he ran into another obstacle: he was broke. After a few months' delay, Colonel A.A. Pope, a prominent manufacturer of bicycles, agreed to back the adventurer, and Stevens sailed for Europe.

The tour through Europe on a bike was quite enjoyable. The sights were interesting; the roads were good; and when his giant front wheel broke down, there was no lack of mechanics who could put the bike back in shape. By early 1885, thousands of Americans were following Stevens' adventure through newspaper accounts.

As Stevens traveled through Persia, India, and the Far East, the trip became more onerous. He was loaded down with gifts from Persian potentates and enthusiastic Chinese villagers.

Mile after mile the tireless Stevens pedaled on. Since he occasionally had to struggle against pranksters and animals who blocked his path on the roads, he refused to make time a factor. On some days he just didn't ride at all; on other days, he moved only by daylight.

But in January of 1887—less than three years after he had left home—Stevens returned, bicycle and all, to San Francisco. He was now famous, and his fame yielded him a considerable income through lectures and writings.

Vidocq, a jailbird, became the world's greatest detective

Eugene François Vidocq was a clever criminal, as well as the outstanding detective of his day. His mysterious and romantic life on both sides of the law have established him as the model of the mastermind sleuth.

Born in 1775, the son of a baker, Vidocq grew up to become a soldier, deserter, hardened criminal, master of escape and disguises, and last of all, in 1809, a police spy for the *Service de Surete*. Later, as head of that detective branch, he was one of the first to investigate crime and criminals through an established procedure, as opposed to the catch-as-catch-can ways of his time. Outlaws often discovered that their "trusted accomplice" turned out to be Vidocq himself, in a completely convincing disguise.

After serving for 23 years in the *Sureté*, the famed sleuth was removed as its head in 1832, charged with instigating a crime so that he might gain praise for uncovering it. For the remaining 25 years of his life, Vidocq ran a paper mill, employing ex-criminals for his work force.

Lola Montez, the dance-hall girl who toppled a king

Marie Delores Eliza Rosanna Gilbert was born poor in Limerick, Ireland, in 1818. After an unsuccessful marriage to an army officer, she adopted the name Lola Montez, invented a line of ancestors from Seville, and headed for Paris to try her luck on the stage.

Although her singing and dancing were not outstanding, Lola's sultry beauty was. She became a star. Among her numerous stage-door Johnnies were Franz Liszt and Alexandre Dumas père.

Lola's reputation soon piqued the interest of King Ludwig I of Bavaria. The impassioned 60-year-old ruler dispatched agents to France with billets-doux and a casket of jewels.

At that moment, Lola was between lovers. Besides, she had never had a king, so she did not resist the royal summons. Lola soon became not only Ludwig's lover, but his chief political advisor as well.

But the burghers of Munich resented the idea that they were being governed by a courtesan, and marched in the streets shouting, "Down with the whore!" In 1848, Lola had the good sense to flee to

Switzerland, just in time to miss the revolution she had helped provoke. Her royal paramour was forced to abdicate.

This interlude with Ludwig did wonders for Lola's stage career. Thousands flocked to see the woman for whose favors a king had lost his throne. And when Lola's fortunes started to decline in Europe, she sailed for New York.

There her racy "Spider Dance" proved a sensation. From there, Lola headed west to San Francisco, then to Australia, and from there back to Europe for a final tour.

Her beauty gone, Lola lived her last years in obscure poverty in New York. She died in 1861, only 43 years old, and was buried in an unmarked grave in Brooklyn's Greenwood Cemetery.

The baby without a brain

On May 26, 1788, a 26-year-old woman named Mary Clark gave birth in the Carlisle Dispensary, England. The child was perfectly developed, except for a somewhat soft head. The doctor passed this off, since the child cried, kicked, ate, and otherwise behaved quite normally; moreover, a baby's head is normally rather soft.

After five days, inexplicably, the infant died. An autopsy revealed the startling fact that the child's skull contained neither a cerebrum, nor a cerebellum, nor a medulla—in short, *no brain*.

Incredible as this case may seem, it is not the only instance of a human being living without a brain. In 1935, another such child was born in St. Vincent's Hospital in New York City. Just like the Clark child, this babe acted normally for the days of its life—27.

The cause of death was unknown until an autopsy revealed that the infant's head contained nothing but water.

Wandering John Chapman planted apple trees for 44 years

John Chapman—better known as Johnny Appleseed—was born in Springfield, Massachusetts, in 1774. Little is known for certain about his early years, except that he was in Pennsylvania in the mid 1790's, distributing apple seeds and saplings to families bound for the West.

In 1801, Johnny appeared in Licking County, Ohio, with a sack of apple seeds he'd collected from cider mills in Pennsylvania and New York. From then until his death in 1845, Johnny Appleseed covered more than 100,000 square miles with apple trees. He retraced his paths over and over again to cultivate and prune the trees he'd planted.

Along the way, Johnny drew attention with his eccentric garb—a coffee sack for a shirt and a tin pot for a hat, in which he would cook his meals. This was fine with him—he distributed Bibles as well as seeds.

Johnny Appleseed was a folk hero in his own day, and his legend seems to have grown with the passage of time. The orchards which dot the eastern United States today are a memorial to his love for the land and for his fellow man.

Huang Erh-nan painted with his tongue

A celebrated Chinese artist of the 1920's, Huang Erh-nan, painted lotus flowers and butterflies on silk. But it was not the subject matter of his art that made Huang so unbelievable; it was his technique. Huang Erh-nan used his tongue as a paint brush, and his mouth as the receptacle for black ink.

The Peking artist first filled his maw with the thick ink Oriental artists prefer for their finest work. Then he leaned over the fine silk cloth he had stretched out on a table, and brushed in his paintings—paintings noted for their delicacy and charm.

Banvard painted a canvas three miles long

In 1840, a 25-year-old New Yorker by the name of John Banvard set out on the Mississippi River in a skiff. For the next 400 days, he rowed and poled his craft along the river, busily sketching the scenery. Thus began the most monumental journey in the history of painting.

Over the next five years, Banvard worked diligently on "The Panorama of the Mississippi," as he named his work. Depicting 1,200 miles of landscape from the mouth of the great river to New Orleans, the work was painted on a grand canvas: 16,000 feet long and 12 feet wide.

The enormous painting was exhibited on two upright revolving cylinders. Despite the fact that it took two hours to view the entire "Panorama," thousands gladly paid to see this sensation. Banvard's colossus earned $200,000 in its tours of leading cities in the United States and Europe. Subsequently, it was sold to an Englishman. Then it vanished.

Garfield could write two languages at the same time

James A. Garfield, 20th President of the United States, was, like Lincoln, born in a log cabin. But by hard work and real ability, he became the head of Hiram Institute, a Major General during the Civil War, a leader in Congress, and finally Chief Executive of the United States.

Like many other people, the well-educated former backwoodsman was ambidextrous. That is to say, he was capable of writing with either his left hand or his right. But Garfield was probably unique in being able to write the two classical languages—Latin and Greek—at the *same* time, one with his right hand, the other with his left!

Ferdinand Waldo Demera, "The Great Imposter"

Ferdinand Waldo Demera saw no reason why his lack of a high-school diploma should stand between him and a professional career. So, through ingenious deceptions and a lot of *chutzpah*, Demera opened the doors that society had closed in his face.

Knowing he would need an impressive resume and references, Demera compiled a fanciful history of previous jobs, and wrote his own references under fictitious or forged signatures.

During the Korean War, Demera somehow found his way onto a Royal Canadian ship as Surgeon Lieutenant. He had had no previous training in medicine. Nevertheless, when he was called upon to operate—and he operated on 19 soldiers during his stay—he acquitted himself well, as Canadian military records indicate.

Another highlight of Demera's career was the time he spent as a professor of applied psychology at several colleges. Passing himself off as a Ph.D., he was academically respected and well-liked by students, faculty, and administration at each school he fooled.

When Demera's academic con game was exposed, he dipped out of sight for a few years before turning up as a guidance counselor for inmates at a Texas prison. Once again, he performed admirably while thumbing his nose at the professional requirements for training.

No institution ever brought criminal proceedings against Demera, knowing that its own reputation would suffer more than Demera's. A Hollywood movie was made of Demera's life more than a decade ago, and since then he has dropped out of sight. But no one knows for sure that he will not strike again—or that he is not out there at this moment, poking fun at some pillar of the Establishment.

William Beckford, the mad builder of towers

William Beckford was but a child when he inherited his father's West Indies plantation, a million pounds, and a sumptuous estate in Wiltshire, England. His guardian saw to it that he obtained the finest education possible. On the Continent, he learned piano from Mozart, and Arabic and Persian from private tutors.

In 1786, at the age of 26, Beckford wrote an Arabian romance called *Vathek* which was greatly admired by Byron, and is still studied in universities today. For some unknown reason, the English-born Beckford wrote his book in French, *and then hired someone to translate it into English*, the language in which it was first published.

In Beckford's novel, an Arabian sultan named Vathek builds an enormous tower, hoping to fathom the secrets of the universe through a study of astrology. In the 1790's, the sultan's preoccupation in the novel became Beckford's preoccupation in reality. Beckford hired England's greatest architect of the time, James Wyatt, to build him a tower as magnificent as Vathek's.

Beckford was terribly impatient for Fonthill Abbey, as he named the structure, to be completed. He had 500 men working on the job night and day, in two shifts. He pressed the workers so hard that they were compelled to take many structural shortcuts.

In 1800, the 300-foot tower was completed. Beckford prepared to move in. But not one week after the tower was completed, the first mild zephyr broke it in half, and reduced the structure to rubble.

Beckford went to work again, this time determined that his tower would *not* fall. He invested seven years and 273,000 pounds to erect it. For 15 years, Beckford lived in this 300-foot tower, until financial reverses forced him to sell it to a man named John Farquhar. Not long after Farquhar moved in, the tower collapsed in a gale.

Beckford's next and last construction was the maddest of his career. On a hill outside the resort town of Bath, Beckford built a modest tower of 130 feet, and stocked it with dwarfs. By now, the middle-aged Beckford had acquired a considerable aversion to women, which he formalized in stone. He had special niches constructed in the hallways, so that his maids could hide themselves when they heard his approach.

She worshipped her husband's heart

History can boast few more dedicated—or more morbid—lovers than Marguerite-Thérèse, Marquise de Vaubrun. Not even the death of her husband could put a dent in her affections.

Upon learning of the Marquis' demise in the battle of Altenheim, Germany, on July 30, 1675, Marguerite-Thérèse swiftly arranged to have his heart returned to her in France. She then had this unusual memento embalmed and encased in glass. For the remaining 29 years of her life, Marguerite-Thérèse spent seven hours a day gazing adoringly at her husband's heart.

Harbo and Samuelson rowed across the Atlantic Ocean

Only two men in all history have ever crossed the Atlantic Ocean by boat with only their own brawny arms for power. On June 6, 1896, George Harbo and Frank Samuelson rowed out of New York harbor in a boat only 18 feet long, with no sail to push it along nor mast to cling to in a raging storm. But they did take along five pairs of oars, 60 gallons of water, and plenty of canned goods.

And so Harbo and Samuelson, choosing a route just south of that generally plied by steamships, steered for Le Havre, France, 3,250 miles away from New York. Each man put in 18 hours a day at the oars. Five hours a day were allowed for rest and one hour a day for eating. They generally rested during the daytime, preferring to do their hard labor during the cool hours of the night. They had planned a schedule of 54 miles a day, and they kept to it.

On July 15, a freighter took the men on board for a short respite, gave the two seafarers some fresh food, and sped them on their way. At this time, the rowing mariners decided they would do better if they headed for England. And so they did, shortening their trip by about 200 miles.

On August 1, 56 days after leaving New York, Harbo and Samuelson rowed onto a quiet coast of the Isles of Scilly, England. There were no cheering throngs to greet them.

Yogi Haridas was buried alive for 40 days

The world's record for the longest live burial is 101 days. But when Mrs. Emma Smith of England attained that mark in 1968, she had air, food, and drink piped into her eight-foot coffin, and she was able to chat with those above ground by means of a closed-circuit television hookup.

By contrast, when Yogi Haridas was buried in Lahore, Punjab, in 1837, he was left *completely unattended* for 40 days. He did not eat, he did not drink, he did not breathe. The Yogi had attained a catatonic trance known as *samadai*—suspended animation. When he was dug up after 40 days, his assistants revived him, with little difficulty, and Yogi Haridas went on to live for many more years.

Da Vinci was the greatest genius of his age

Given a choice, which would you prefer to be—painter, sculptor, architect, musician, poet or philosopher? Or perhaps you'd prefer to be an inventor, a biologist, an astronomer, a geologist, or a mathematician? Imagine a man whose genius permitted him to become all these things, and a master in every one of these disciplines! Such was the incredible Leonardo da Vinci.

Born near Florence, Italy, in 1452, Leonardo—while still a schoolboy—solved complicated mathematical problems that stumped his teachers. In his teens, he was apprenticed to the noted painter, Andrea del Verrocchio. By the age of 20, the student had equaled his master!

While still in his early 30's, Leonardo painted the famed "Last Supper," the giant tableau which, though its colors have faded with time, ranks as one of the world's supreme art masterpieces. Not long after, he painted another immortal, the "Mona Lisa," perhaps the most famous painting in the world.

In middle age, Leonardo created many of the beautiful decorations in the Pope's Palaces of the Vatican and in St. Peter's Basilica in Rome.

During his lifetime, Leonardo won renown almost exclusively as an artist; yet his notebooks contain scores of sketches of fantastic inventions, anticipating scientific creations that were not to be created for centuries to come. Indeed, most of Leonardo's brainchildren—such as the airplane, the helicopter, and the submarine—were laughed at during his lifetime, and were forgotten until modern science rediscovered them.

The most astounding child prodigy ever

Christian Friedrich Heinecken was born in Lubeck, Germany, in 1721. Within eight weeks of his birth, Christian was speaking intelligible German. At the age of one, he read the Pentateuch. Next year, between the ages of two and three, he familiarized himself with the entire Bible, both the Old and New Testaments.

In his third year, Christian devoted himself to the study of history and geography, and learned to read both French and Latin.

Word of the boy's prodigious intellect swept Europe, and the King of Denmark invited Christian to demonstrate his acumen at the royal residence in Copenhagen.

Powerful as Christian's intelligence was, his body was amazingly weak. His tiny fingers lacked the strength to even grasp a pen, and he was utterly unable to eat solid food. At the age of four, Little Christian predicted his imminent death. Unfortunately, he was correct.

Vergil spent $100,000 on the burial of a fly

The Roman poet Vergil (70 B.C.-19 B.C.) is universally recognized as one of the greatest literary artists the world has ever known. He wrote the masterful *Eclogues* and *Georgics*, but his fame rests principally upon the *Aeneid*.

Besides being a supreme poet, Vergil was a fascinating man, with an incredible flair for the bizarre. For example, read of this incident reported by Suetonius Tranquillis in his *Life of Augustus*.

When Rome was placed under the rule of the Second Triumvirate (Augustus, Marc Antony, and Lepidus) in 43 B.C., the lands of the idle rich were ordered confiscated and allotted to war veterans. Certain grounds were exempted from this ordinance, such as cemetery plots and mausoleums.

Fearing that his manor on the Esquiline Hill in Rome would be taken from him, Vergil conceived a brilliant ploy. In his house, he staged an elaborate funeral for a fly which he claimed to be his dearly beloved pet. Various Roman dignitaries delivered mournful orations, as did Vergil, and the fly was interred amid splendid trappings costing more than 800,000 sesterces—the equivalent of well over $100,000 today.

Vergil's outlandish rites for his "pet" fly transformed his home into a "mausoleum," thus saving it from the hands of the government.

Frenchwoman Renée Bordereau fought in 200 battles

During the French Revolution of 1789, many people in the provinces refused to side with the rebels. In the vanguard of those faithful to the King were the people of the Vendée, in western France. They rose against the Revolutionary regime in 1793, and for six years fought to restore the Bourbons to the throne.

The great heroine of this revolt was Renee Bordereau, sometimes called "The Second Joan of Arc." Renee's father was killed before her eyes by revolutionary soldiers, and at the age of 23 she enlisted in the Vendéean army.

Dressed as a man, she always led the attack and sought the most dangerous posts. Renée's comrades-in-arms, who did not for a moment suspect that she was a woman, greatly admired her courage.

Even after the Vendéean revolt had been put down by Napoleon, he feared to permit Renée to remain at liberty lest she lead a new rebellion. Instead, he put a price of 40 million francs on her head. She was captured, and Napoleon had her imprisoned for five years.

Two years after the final overthrow of Napoleon in 1815, Renée Bordereau was received with honors at the court of the French king, Louis XVIII.

William Northmore lost $850,000 on the turn of a card

William Northmore (1690-1735) of Okehampton, England, was an inveterate gambler. Cards were what he loved best, but he'd just as soon bet on the horses, or on votes in Parliament.

After several years of stunning success, he met his downfall in the form of an ace of diamonds. With the turn of that one card, his entire fortune of $850,000 was wiped out. Northmore vowed never to gamble another penny, but his promise was somewhat hollow, for he had nary a penny to gamble with.

Lady Luck soon smiled on the beggared young man, not at the gaming tables, but at the polls. The townspeople of Okehampton, in sympathy for Northmore's plight, elected him to Parliament in 1714, and in every election thereafter until his death 19 years later.

William Miller merchandised Doomsday

William Miller (1782-1849) was the founder of the sect known as the Second Adventists, or Millerites. In 1831, he made the first of his more than 3,200 speeches predicting the second coming of Christ in 1843.

The Massachusetts prophet of earthly doom turned a fast buck on his prophesies. To those wishing to ready themselves for Judgment Day, he sold muslin "ascension robes."

When 1843 passed with no undue commotion, Miller revised his Doomsday prediction to 1844. After another uneventful year, Miller and his followers met in Albany, New York, to reassess their timetable. Circumspectly, the gathering of Millerites declared its belief in the return of Christ at an indefinite time.

Mohammed III began his reign by killing 19 brothers

In 1595, Mohammed III of Turkey (1567-1603) became sultan of the Ottoman Empire. Under his father, Murad III, the Turkish grasp on the empire had begun to slip as the sultan was dominated by his harem. Even though Murad's generals managed to win some decisive battles before his death, his son Mohammed recognized that for him, the throne would be a very precarious perch.

With a ruthlessness spurred by stark terror, Mohammed tried to solidify his hold on the empire through fratricide. One of his first acts as sultan was to order the execution of 19 of his brothers, thus serving a warning to anyone else who might have had visions of a coup. For all his bloodthirsty machinations, Mohammed III ruled only eight years before joining his 19 brothers in death.

Emperor Sutoku penned a book with his own blood

During the twelfth century, Sutoku, Emperor of Japan, was sent into exile for three years. He passed this long period copying the *Lankauarn Sutra*, a Buddhist religious work, in red ink—his own blood!

The emperor's book totaled 135 pages containing 10,500 words. Sutoku hoped that his patient efforts would not go unrewarded—that Buddha, his diety, would return him to the Japanese throne. History records that Sutoku *did* return to power again in 1144 and ruled Japan for two more decades.

Houdini stayed underwater in a sealed coffin an hour-and-a half

No locks, no chains, no manacles could hold Harry Houdini, the greatest escape artist of all time. Born as Erich Weiss in 1874, this boy from Appleton, Wisconsin, did not take long to make headlines.

His handcuff act became so famous that he was invited to "escape" from London's Scotland Yard. Superintendent Melville, chief of this institution, placed Houdini's arms around a pillar and then handcuffed him. Before Melville was out of the building, Houdini had freed himself and caught up to the chief!

Houdini could open any lock in the world in a few minutes. Once, on a tour through Europe, the continent's most famous locksmiths presented him with what they considered foolproof locks, the result of countless years of work. Houdini opened the locks so astonishingly fast that the master mechanics hardly knew what was happening.

During his European tour, Houdini escaped from jails in the cities of Liverpool, Amsterdam, Moscow, and The Hague. He duplicated these feats in almost every large city in the United States. The plain fact was that Houdini could enter or leave virtually any room, building, or cell at will.

His repertoire of escape acts fascinated millions all over the world. So uncanny were his performances that many believed Houdini possessed supernatural powers. Though Houdini vociferously denied being gifted with anything more than human attributes, his performances were so baffling that even his stout denials failed to squelch the talk. No one could fathom just how his stunts were accomplished; and it was not until after his death that his notebooks revealed how he contrived to do things which seemed beyond the powers of mortals.

One of his favorite stunts was to have himself bound by the police in a straitjacket used for the violently insane. No one, the police averred, could break out of this. But, in addition to the straitjacket, Harry had the police load him with iron shackles and ropes. Houdini was turned upside down, and hauled aloft in mid-air by means of a block and pulley. Then, in full sight of an astounded audience and an absolutely dumbfounded police detail, the incredible man would wriggle free.

How did he do it?

Houdini was one of the greatest athletes that

ever lived. From his early youth on, he had practiced body control. He could flex virtually every muscle in his body. His fingers had the strength of pliers; and his teeth were so strong that they could be used like a can opener. His strength was so great that he could bend iron bars, and his tactile sensibility so fantastic that while blindfolded he could tell the exact number of toothpicks he was kneeling on.

Still, how did Houdini get out of that straitjacket? Answer: He contracted his muscles in such a way that he could slip one hand out of its bonds. By similar contractions and maneuverings, he would set his limbs free. Then the great magician would free himself from his iron fetters.

Houdini left explicit directions as to just how the stunt could be accomplished, but so far no athlete has come along with enough physical dexterity to perform the feat.

Unsurpassed as a magician, Houdini displayed courage and daring equally unmatched. In the days when the airplane was still a new and unproved machine, Houdini jumped from one airplane to another—3,000 feet above the earth—*while handcuffed!*

On August 26, 1907, Houdini leaped off a bridge in San Francisco Bay with his hands tied

behind his back and 75 pounds of ball and chain attached to his body. He came up out of the water unharmed.

On another occasion, Houdini was thrown into the East River in New York City, handcuffed inside a box to which 200 pounds of irons had been attached. But what were handcuffs, irons, and a river to Harry? He emerged within two minutes.

And then, on August 5, 1926, as if to cap all his former feats, he allowed himself to be sealed in a coffin which was then lowered into the waters of a swimming pool. Before a whole deputation of doctors and newsmen, he remained in the coffin under water *a full hour and a half!*

Immediately upon emerging, he was examined by physicians who all agreed that he had suffered no ill effects. Houdini contended that it was panic, not lack of air, which usually caused suffocation. His own muscle control was so phenomenal that he may have accomplished this stunt by means of suspended animation.

Yet despite the fact that the physicians gave Houdini a clean bill of health on August 5, 1926, the great magician and athlete did not live to see 1927.

Cunningham, despite a toeless foot, became a great track star

As an eight-year-old, Glenn Cunningham was trapped in a terrible fire. Before the boy could escape from the flames, his left foot was horribly burned. All the toes were lost as well as much of the muscle tissue. His doctors broke the bad news gently to young Glenn: they told him he could never hope to walk again.

But Glenn refused to heed those grim words. He worked hard at getting well, and he learned to walk once more. Next, he learned to run. In fact, he ran so well that he became a great track star, first in high school and then at the University of Kansas. He set world records in the mile, both indoors and outdoors. Glenn's indoor mile in 4 minutes 4 and 4/10 seconds, achieved in 1938, stood as a world record for many years.

The world's greatest inventor

Thomas Alva Edison was born in Milan, Ohio in 1837. Seven years later, his family moved to Huron, Michigan, and young Tom took a fling at formal schooling. That lasted but a scant three months; by then, Thomas Edison had seen the inside of a schoolhouse for the last time.

Edison went to work as a newsboy on the Grand Trunk Railroad. As he grew older, he graduated to the position of telegraph operator. It was this experience which prompted his first invention: a transmitter-receiver for the automatic telegraph, and the quadruplex method of sending out four telegraph messages simultaneously.

In his long life, Thomas Alva Edison invented:

1. An electric vote recorder.

2. Paraffin paper.

3. An improved stock ticker system.

4. An electric pen which was later developed into the mimeograph.

5. The carbon telephone transmitter which made Bell's telephone commercially successful; it also laid the groundwork for today's microphone.

6. The phonograph.

7. The first practical electric light.

8. Electric generators, motors, light sockets, and other components of a complete electrical power system.

9. An efficient electric storage battery.

10. Many components of an electric railway system, including the automatic signal.

11. The dictating machine.

He also developed:

1. The first practical typewriter.

2. The vacuum tube that made modern radio and television possible.

3. A motion picture camera and sound system that prepared the way for talking pictures.

4. Synthetic rubber.

At his death in 1931, Edison held over 1,300 U.S. and foreign copyrights!

Gama, a 5-foot 7-inch Indian, was the greatest wrestler in history

Although much smaller than most wrestlers you see on TV, Gama of Patala, India, made up for his size, and then some. Generally acknowledged to be the top wrestler of all time, this 5-foot 7-inch, 260-pound battler had a hard time finding competition. Most wrestlers feared Gama so much they would not enter the ring with him. Gama reigned as world champ well into his fifties.

In London in 1910, the Indian challenged any 20 wrestlers to meet him in combat, promising to throw them all in succession within an hour. But the Britons wouldn't take on the Indian terror. Indeed, throughout his career, Gama was able to lure only two Occidentals to do battle with him. One was an American named B.F. Roller; the other a Pole, the world-famous professional wrestler Stanislaus Zbysko, a gigantic hunk of a man, and generally regarded by sports writers as a very competent athlete. Neither lasted more than half a minute.

A Knoxville baby had a nine-inch tail

Throughout recorded history, there have been legends of people born with full-grown tails. Upon investigation, however, such stories have all turned out to be myths.

Yet in 1928, at a hospital in Knoxville, Tennessee, a baby was born with a tail that measured nine inches in length.

A grandmother at 17

At the age of seven, Mum-zi joined the harem of Chief Akkiri, ruler of the estuary of Calabar, Nigeria. Shortly after her betrothal, Mum-zi became pregnant. At the age of eight years and four months, she gave birth to a perfectly normal, well-developed child.

When the daughter of Mum-zi and Akkiri also gave birth at the age of eight, Mum-zi became a grandma at age 17—the youngest grandmother on record.

Philippe Petit, tightrope artist at 110 stories up

Early one morning in August, 1974, the skyline of lower Manhattan was altered in a small but stunning way: the twin towers of the World Trade Center, second tallest building in the world, were linked by a one-inch steel cable—and perched on that cable was a fellow named Philippe Petit. For 45 minutes, this 25-year-old French acrobat and juggler thrilled thousands of Manhattanites as he danced in mid-air at the dizzying height of 1,350 feet.

When Philippe grew bored with life at the top, he put his feet down on firmer terra and was promptly arrested for disorderly conduct. To police and newsmen, Petit made it clear that his conduct was, for him, the very model of order. In fact, his high-wire antics 110 stories up were the culmination of 10 years' study and practice.

At the age of 15, Philippe quit school and joined the Omankowsky acrobatic troupe in the Loire Valley. In 1971, he became a celebrity in France by walking a high wire strung between the towers of Notre Dame cathedral. Shortly thereafter, he traveled to Sydney, Australia, and traversed a

cable from one pylon of the giant Harbour Bridge
to the other.

Petit's boldest venture required six months'
study of the World Trade Center. He rented an
apartment in New York and, with the help of

friends, "cased the joint." Often, he and his friends had to don hard hats or pose as French architectural reporters to mask their real purpose. At last, in August 1974, they hid in one tower overnight and, with a crossbow, shot their cable across to the other tower. The next morning, Petit took his stratospheric stroll.

A reporter asked Petit the inevitable question: why did he do it? "I see three oranges," Petit responded, "I have to juggle. I see two towers, I have to walk."

Hedley fell out of his plane and, hundreds of feet below, fell back into it

On January 6, 1918, Captain J.H. Hedley, an American, was flying 15,000 feet over German territory in a plane piloted by a Canadian named Makepeace. Suddenly, their craft was attacked by German fighters. Trying to evade the enemy, Makepeace took his plane into a nearly vertical dive. The suddenness of this maneuver surprised Hedley, who was pulled out of his seat and off into the ozone.

Makepeace gave his comrade up for lost, and continued his rapid descent for several hundred feet more before leveling off. Then, incredibly, Hedley alighted on the tail of the airplane! Evidently, the steep dive had created a powerful suction in which the American captain was caught.

Hedley hung on to the tail of the plane for dear life. Later, he managed to climb back into his seat. The plane touched down safely behind Allied lines, and Hedley's reprieve from death was complete.

Sanson was Chief Executioner at the age of seven

In France during the early eighteenth century, the job of Chief Executioner was handed down from father to son. Thus, when the elder Charles-Jean-Baptiste Sanson passed away in 1726, his son Charles automatically assumed the post—even though he was only seven years old.

At that time, prisoners condemned to death were decapitated. Since young Charles was not

yet strong enough to handle the heavy executioner's sword, he was permitted to employ a "helper" named Prudhomme who actually wielded the blade. But little Charles had to be present at every execution, for he was the only one authorized to put the official seal to the grim act.

Finally, at the age of 12, the Chief Executioner took on the full reponsibility of his job by chopping off the heads of the condemned himself.

Spinola, "Father of French Ballet," had no legs

For true grit, few stories can match that of Sebastien Spinola. The 16th-century Frenchman lost both legs to the surgeon at the age of 11, yet went on to live a full life as a dancing master! Today, he is generally accorded the title of the "Father of the French Ballet."

Milo of Crotona, strong man and philosopher

The greatest wrestler and strong man of the ancient world was a Greek named Milo. He hailed from the southern Italian city of Croton, a Greek colony founded in the 8th century B.C. by settlers from Achaea. He is more commonly known by the Latin form of his name: Milo of Crotona.

Milo was a man of diversified interests and attainments. Skilled as a soldier and singer, he was a favorite disciple of the famous philosopher-mathematician Pythagoras, and he was himself the author of the *Physica*, a book on science and natural history. But above all, Milo was renowned as an athlete. His specialties were wrestling and feats of strength.

Milo won the wrestling championship at each of the six meetings of Olympic Games between 540 and 516 B.C. He was the only man in the history of the ancient Olympics (776 B.C. to A.D. 393) to win so many victories in any sport. Milo's achievement becomes even more impressive when one notes that his active career as a wrestler covered more than 24 years, an extremely long time for an athlete to maintain himself at championship peak.

Milo's amazing feats are recorded in the writings of such reliable ancient historians as

Pausanias, Plutarch, and Strabo. According to

their reports, Milo's fingers were so powerful that no one could bend them when he extended his hand horizontally. On one occasion, Milo enclosed a tender pomegranate in his mighty fist. Scores of other athletes tried to get it away from him but none succeeded. When Milo finally opened his hand, there was not the slightest bruise on the fruit.

Milo is best known, however, for a feat he performed on the opening day of one of the meetings of the Olympic Games. Carrying a full-grown ox on his shoulders—the ox must have weighed at least a ton—Milo strolled effortlessly into the stadium at Olympia. Before the amazed eyes of thousands, he carried the ox across the playing field. The story goes on to say that he slaughtered the ox, which he may have, but the legend that he ate all the meat on that same day seems apocryphal.

Tragically, it was Milo's incredible strength that proved to be his doom. Walking in the wilds one day, Milo chanced upon a tree whose trunk was partially split. Never one to turn away from a challenge, the giant tried to rip the parts asunder. However, Milo's hand became caught in the tree trunk and, with no companion to free him, Milo was devoured that night by wolves.

The lady who left her fortune to snowmen

A few days after the death of Madame de la Bresse, a prim Parisian noted for her eccentric ways, her lawyer called in the family and friends for the reading of the will. The testament was brief and unambiguous: all 125,000 francs were to go toward providing the snowmen of Paris with clothing, for the sake of decency!

The will was contested by those whose great expectations had been shattered. In court, they maintained that at the time the Madame formulated the will, in 1876, she was not in possession of her wits.

Perhaps in admiration for the way Madame de la Bresse had foiled these vultures, the Judge declined to overturn the terms of her will. Paris, the world's capital of fashion, was to have the world's best-dressed snowmen.

Firdausi wrote a single poem, 2,804 pages long

The classic Persian poet of the tenth century, Firdausi, spent 35 of his more than 80 years writing the *Shah Namah*. This great poem, known as "The Book of Kings," is 2,804 pages long. Its 120,000 lines—60,000 couplets—are contained in nine good-sized volumes, making it the lengthiest poem ever written by one poet. The poem describes the history of Persia and Persia's monarchs from earliest times, 700 years before the birth of Christ, to the period of the Arabian conquest in the seventh century A.D.

According to a tale handed down through the centuries, Firdausi was cheated by the Persian sultan, Mahmud of Ghazni. Mahmud, it seems, had agreed to give Firdausi a piece of gold for every couplet the poet wrote. But when the time for payment came, the sultan sought to give the poet silver instead. Firdausi refused to accept the silver coins and shortly turned his pen against the Sultan, deriding him with sharp satire for not having kept his word. As a result, Mahmud angrily condemned the man to death. But before the sentence could be carried out, Firdausi fled the realm.

With the passage of time the sultan relented. When he learned that Firdausi in his old age was returning to his native land, the ruler arranged the long overdue debt. But it was too late. The royal elephant, burdened with 60,000 gold pieces, arrived just after the poet had died.

Queen Kahena had a harem of 400 husbands

Women's lib is nothing new to the Berbers of Northwest Africa. Their famous Queen Kahena of Aures, Algeria, had a harem of 400 male concubines.

The "Scottish Brothers" had one body and two heads

In the late 15th century, the court of James III of Scotland featured one of the oddities of the age—the "Scottish Brothers." When young King James learned of a set of twins joined at the abdomen, with two legs, four arms, and two heads, he had the children sent to the royal court. James wanted not only to satisfy his curiosity, but also to save the freaks from possible harm in the rural backwater from which they came.

King James arranged for the "Scottish Brothers" to be educated, including special training in art, music, and foreign languages. As the brothers matured, they each developed passionate and sometimes contrary tastes in music, art, and letters. These antagonisms often reached the point of physical mayhem. The sight of the brothers' four fists raining blows upon their two heads must have looked like a helicopter.

The brothers lived under royal protection for the rest of their lives, until they were 28. One brother died five days before the other, who moaned piteously as he crept about the castle gardens, half dead and half alive.

Geoffrey Hudson was 18 inches tall at the age of 30

Georges Buffon, the great French naturalist of the 18th century, recorded the story of a dwarf who, at the age of 37, was only 16 inches tall. But the smallest adult dwarf about whom we have more complete information was Geoffrey Hudson.

Hudson was born in Oakham, England, in 1619. When he was eight years old and not quite 14 inches tall, he popped out of a pie at the table of King Charles I and Queen Henrietta-Maria. In the next 22 years, Geoffrey grew only four more inches, to the height of a foot and a half. (In his remaining years, however, he more than doubled his size, shooting up to 3'9".)

Hudson was a great favorite of the Queen, who once sent him to her native France to obtain a midwife for the impending royal birth. While there, Geoffrey was insulted by a haughty French official; much to the Frenchman's amusement, the dwarf challenged him to a duel. The amusement was as short-lived as the official himself. At dawn the next day, Geoffrey killed him with one shot.

Back in England, the little man with the big heart engaged in another duel. This time the "insult" was perpetrated by a turkey who happened to filch the Lilliputian's lunch. Enraged, Hudson took on the turkey in a battle to the death. With much difficulty, since the gobbler was considerably taller and heavier, Geoffrey emerged the victor. In revenge for his lost lunch, he ate the loser.

Lope de Vega wrote more than 1,500 plays

Felix Lope de Vega Carpio, the renowned Spanish dramatic poet born in 1562, wrote an estimated 1,500 plays—not to speak of countless poems, epics, and prose works. Of these 1,500 plays, about 500 survive.

De Vega penned his first drama at the age of 11, while a student at a Jesuit school. From that moment on, he poured out a torrent of theatrical works the like of which has never been equaled.

Barclay walked 1,000 miles in 1,000 hours—one mile every hour

Captain Allardyce Barclay of Ury, Scotland, was veritably a man with "asbestos feet." At age 17, he could walk six miles an hour. At age 27, he claimed that he could walk 1,000 miles in 1,000 hours. A group of Englishmen didn't believe this incredible Scot, and offered odds of 100 to 1 against Barclay's boast.

On June 1, 1809, Barclay lined up ready to go the distance. The terms of the wager called for him to walk one mile within each of the next consecutive 1,000 hours. The mile was to be covered regardless of weather. The hours were to be counted uninterruptedly. He would be obliged to walk one-half mile down a path from his own lodgings in Newmarket and then walk the same half-mile back to his home. Barclay had undertaken a stint that would keep him going without a decent sleep for roughly six weeks. It seemed utterly impossible that any man would have the endurance to do this.

Surprisingly, the lack of rest was not the Captain's major problem. Barclay devised a system of walking the first mile at the very end of a rest period. He then immediately commenced to do a second mile at the very beginning of the following hour. Since each mile took him approximately 15 minutes, this arrangement permitted him to rest for several 1½-hour periods each day. But Barclay began suffering from muscle spasms and blisters. Moreover, there was grave concern that the wearied contestant might be the victim of foul play on the dark road, for a good deal of money was being bet against him. His brother arranged to have the pathway lit at night.

During those summer days, the road became hot and dusty. Ingeniously, Barclay had a water cart sprinkle the path in front of him. In between times, he cheerfully indulged in solid meals of mutton chops and beefsteaks, washed down by generous drafts of port.

At the start, Barclay required approximately 13 minutes for each mile; but after four weeks of steady perambulating, he was worn to a frazzle. As he plowed through his miles in 20 minutes each, the odds against him grew. But Barclay, half-dead, struggled on.

Strangely enough, as he approached the finish, he actually gained strength. During the last few days, ropes were needed to hold back the crowd, and lords and commoners filled every available room in the Newmarket area. Many were bettors

who, in the aggregate, had staked $500,000 on Barclay's trial of endurance.

On July 12, Barclay finished his last mile. The final chore took him a mere 15 minutes, and he wound up 45 minutes ahead of schedule. It was like dashing for a pot of gold, for he had bet a very considerable sum on himself. In winning, Barclay became a wealthy man.

Max Hoffman, the American Lazarus

In 1865, in a small town in Wisconsin, five-year-old Max Hoffman came down with cholera. Three days later, the doctor pulled the sheets over the boy's head and pronounced him dead.

Little Max was laid to rest in the village cemetery. That night, his mother awoke screaming: she had dreamt that her son was turning over in his coffin, trying to escape. Trembling with fear, she begged her husband to go to the cemetery immediately and raise the coffin. Mr. Hoffman did his best to calm his wife, assuring her that while her nightmare was indeed hideous, it was still just a dream. Assuaged, Mrs. Hoffman returned to bed.

But the next night, Max's mother had the identical dream, and this time she would not be denied. Resignedly, Mr. Hoffman asked his eldest boy and a neighbor to help him exhume the corpse. They dug up the coffin, opened the lid, and incredibly, there was Max, lying *on his side!* Though he showed no signs of life, Mr. Hoffman brought the boy back to the house so the doctor could have one last look at him.

At the Hoffman home, the physician labored to revive him. After an hour, Max's eyelid fluttered. The doctor immediately placed heated salt bags under the boy's arms, rubbed his lips with brandy, and watched for signs of recovery.

Recover Max did. After a week, he was out playing with his comrades. And the boy who died at five lived well into his 80's in Clinton, Iowa. For his entire life, Max Hoffman's most treasured memento was the metal handles he had taken from his own coffin.

The Earl of Bridgewater dressed his dogs as humans

The Rev. Francis Henry Egerton, Earl of Bridgewater, was a Prince of the Holy Roman Empire, a scholar, and a patron of the arts. In addition, he was enormously wealthy. During the last few years before his death in February, 1829,

Lord Egerton took to heart the adage that a man's best friend is his dog.

Lord Egerton was a permanent resident of the prestigious Hotel de Noailles in Paris. Each night, he would sit down to a formal dinner with a dozen guests—all of them came dressed in the height of fashion. In a Parisian journal of 1826, there is this account of a typical evening with the Earl:

"No less than a dozen favorite dogs...daily partake of milord's dinner, seated very gravely in armchairs, each with a napkin around his neck, and a servant behind to attend to his wants. These honorable quadrupeds, as if grateful for such delicate attentions, comport themselves during the time of repast with a decency and decorum which would do more than honor to a party of gentlemen; but if, by any chance, one of them should without due consideration obey the natural instinct of his appetite, and transgress any of the rules of good manners, his punishment is at hand. The day following the offense, the dog dines, and even dines well; but not at milord's table; banished to the antechamber, and dressed in livery, he eats in sorrow the bread of shame, and picks the bones of mortification, while his place at table remains vacant till his repentance has merited a generous pardon!"

After dinner, Lord Egerton liked to take a fast turn about town in his elegant carriage. For company, he would bring along a pack of his pampered pooches, each outfitted with four tiny boots to protect its paws from the mud of the Paris roadways.

Hetty Green, the millionairess who lived like a pauper

Hetty Green, born in New Bedford, Massachusetts in 1835, inherited a substantial fortune upon her father's death. Managing her investments shrewdly, she eventually built up her father's estate to over 100 million dollars.

Yet for all her riches, Hetty Green lived the life of a pauper. For example, while she and her two children resided in Bellows Falls, Vermont, her son Edward broke his leg. Hetty did not call for a doctor—the expense was too great, she felt—and instead took him to the charity hospital, where she passed herself off as a beggar. Unfortunately, the condition of young Edward's leg steadily worsened, and it became clear that amputation was necessary if the boy's life were to be saved. Hetty had the operation performed in her rooming house, to save the lying-in fee at the hospital.

In her later years, Hetty lived in an unheated tenement and subsisted on a diet of cold eggs and onions, to spare the cost of heating her food. She wore newspapers for underpants.

All the while, her fortune grew. At her death in 1916, Hetty's estate was 125 million dollars!

Poon Lim survived for 133 days on a life raft

On November 23, 1942, the S.S. Lomond, an English merchant ship manned by a crew of 55, was torpedoed in the South Atlantic. Only one of the seamen survived—a 25-year-old Chinese by the name of Poon Lim. He had been catapulted off the deck by an explosion of such force that his clothes were blown from his back.

Lim swam in the neighborhood of the wreck for two hours, and then grabbed a drifting life raft. On this he went on to survive for 133 days, naked and exposed to the elements. The raft carried enough food and water for him to live through 60 days. After that, his very life depended on the fish he could catch.

Poon fashioned a hook from a spring which he extracted from the raft's flashlight, and he trolled for small fish. He used these small ones as bait for larger ones. Occasionally, he would grab at and catch a sea gull for a meatier meal.

But hunger was not his only trial. Verily, Poon Lim was like Coleridge's "ancient mariner," who bemoaned:

Alone, alone, Oh! all alone,
  Alone on a wide, wide sea;
And never a saint took pity on
  My soul in agony.

For more than four months, Lim drifted through calm and squall, and at long last neared the coast of Brazil. On April 5, 1943, he was spotted by some fishermen who took him aboard. He was palpably ill, and his legs were wobbly. His rescuers found it hard to believe that this 5-foot 5-inch little mite of a man could possibly have endured so long on an exposed raft, bobbing at random in the middle of the ocean.

When the story reached Britain, the tale met with a stunned reaction. The British knew about the torpedoing of the S.S. Lomond. King George VI, deeply impressed with Poon's fortitude, presented him in 1943 with England's highest civilian award. Speaking of his incredible record, Poon Lim said: "I hope no one will ever have to break it."

Elijah ben Solomon, the genius rabbi

Elijah ben Solomon (1720-1797) was the Head Rabbi of Lithuania, and the leader of the large Jewish community in Vilna. While he was revered for his piety, his mental powers were such that he was universally known as Elijah the Gaon (the Genius).

Elijah's brain was a library in itself; once he read a book, it was committed to his memory. This required no special effort on his part—it just happened! The Gaon is said to have memorized 2,500 volumes, including all the important Hebrew religious works. From these, he could quote any passage at will.

Louis Cyr, the strongest man in the world

He stood only five feet, ten-and-one-half inches, but his huge chest, which bulged 60 inches in circumference, seemed like a barrel that had popped out of his 300-pound frame. His legs and his biceps were tremendous. The strength of the

farm boy from St. Cyprein, Quebec, is the stuff
that legends are made of.

But Louis Cyr was no legend. He really could
lift a full barrel of cement with one arm, and he
once pushed a freight car on the railroad tracks up
an incline. On another occasion, 18 men, who in
the aggregate weighed 4,300 pounds, stood on a

platform. Louis Cyr lifted the platform. And to get tongues wagging, Cyr lifted 588 pounds off the floor—with one finger!

But undoubtedly, Cyr's most dramatic feat occurred on the day he was pitted against four workhorses. On December 20, 1891, standing before a crowd of 10,000, in Sohmer Park, Montreal, Louis Cyr was fitted with a special harness. Four draft horses were lined up opposite Cyr, a pair of them to his left, and a second pair to his right. Heavy leather straps encased his upper arms; sturdy hooks at the end of these straps were attached to whiffletrees which led to harnesses strapped to the four horses.

Cyr stood with his feet planted wide and placed his arms on his chest. As Louis gave the word, the grooms urged their horses to pull. The regulations of the contest ruled out any sudden jerk. The four horses pulled with all their might and main on the strong man, trying to dislodge Louis' arms from his chest. If Cyr lost his footing or either arm left his chest, he would lose the contest.

The grooms whipped the horses, and urged them in every way to pull harder and harder. But the horses slipped and slid, while Cyr didn't budge an inch. After a few minutes of tugging, it was obvious that Cyr was stronger than all four horses put together.

Mohammed II, a model of ruthlessness

Mohammed II was Sultan of Turkey from 1451 to 1481. His fabulous conquests made the Ottoman Empire the power it was to be for four centuries.

One day, his dinner was interrupted by some pressing affair of state. When he returned to the table, he was much put out to discover that his dessert, a juicy melon, had vanished.

Mohammed was incensed. Immediately, he interrogated fourteen of his royal attendants. Each denied any knowledge of the theft. Determined to reach the bottom of this larceny, Mohammed then ordered his court doctor to slit open the stomach of each of the pages—which the doctor did!

Mohammed's hunch was ill-founded. None of the stomachs bore any trace of melon.

What did the sultan do next?

He apologized, and contented himself with another dessert.

Prince Randion, "The Caterpillar Man"

Prince Randion was born in British Guiana in 1871 without arms or legs. At the age of 18, he was brought to America by P.T. Barnum. Though a medical man would label the Prince a human torso, Randion was known in the circus as "The Caterpillar Man" or "The Snake Man."

Despite his handicap, Prince Randion could write by holding a pencil between his lips, could roll a cigarette, and could shave himself. These last two talents were exhibited in Tod Browning's 1933 movie *Freaks*. Moreover, Prince Randion married and fathered five children.

Salo Finkelstein, the mathematical machine

Some few years before World War II, the Polish Treasury Department began an economy drive by hiring Salo Finkelstein of Warsaw. Dr. Finkelstein merely replaced some 40-odd people, each of whom had operated a calculating machine. And the Polish Government vouched for the fact that during the five years in which Dr. Finkelstein tossed huge columns of figures around in his head, he did not make a single mistake.

For Salo Finkelstein was a genius if ever there was one. You could give him a large number like 3,108, and in less than one minute he would reduce it accurately to the sum of the following squares: 52^2, 16^2, 12^2, and 2^2—a simple little maneuver that would take most of us half-an-hour or more to work out, if we could do it at all. The Doctor could look at an arithmetical problem like $6,894 \times 2,763$, and in just seven seconds, without benefit of paper and pencil, come up with the right answer.

What made Finkelstein such a baffling mystery was his superhuman memory; some people call it a photographic mind. Say that you called out two five-digit numbers to Finkelstein and told him to multiply them together. Remembering the two given numbers was not what made Finkelstein a phenomenon: it was his ability to see all the numbers he was working with just as if they were written down on a huge slate before him. In his public performances, Finkelstein did use a blackboard. He drew a square containing five rows of five spaces, or 25 spaces in all. Then he turned his back to the board.

Folks in the audience came up and filled in the spaces with numbers. Finkelstein turned around and took one quick glance at the blackboard. Then, either blindfolded or with his back turned to the board, he recited the 25 numbers, going from left to right, then going from top to bottom, then moving diagonally, then spirally; or in fact, in any way that you might ask him to juggle his figures. And an hour later, after his mind had been filled with every conceivable sort of calculation, he would repeat those 25 numbers to perfection.

He remembered pi to 300 decimal places. He could recite logarithms from 1 to 100 to the seventh decimal and from 101 to 150 to the fifth decimal. He could conjure up, without a second's hesitation, thousands of square roots, cube roots, products, quotients, and number combinations.

Francesco Lentini had three legs

Francesco A. Lentini was that rare medical phenomenon, the pygomele—a person born with an extra limb growing from the buttocks. Born in Sicily in 1889, Lentini was able to walk and run on all three legs until the age of six, at which time his two normally positioned legs began to outgrow the third.

When Lentini was a mature adult, his extra leg was three inches short of the ground. Nevertheless, Lentini could still move it independently of the other legs, and it was sufficiently strong and coordinated to kick a football.

George Psalmanazar perpetrated the greatest literary hoax of all time

"George Psalmanazar" is the pseudonym adopted by a Frenchman who, in the first years of the 18th century, bamboozled the whole of Europe.

His facility with several languages enabled Psalmanazar—his real name is not known—to travel through Europe posing as a Japanese convert to Christianity. This fraud was quite lucrative, for few Europeans had ever seen a Japanese, and they were willing to pay to do so.

While in Holland in 1702, Psalmanazar's ruse was penetrated by an English army chaplain named William Innes. Innes, however, did not expose the Frenchman. He agreed to keep his discovery to himself, provided that Psalmanazar would go to England as a "Formosan" convert to Christianity, giving credit for the exotic conversion to Chaplain Innes.

Since the isle of Formosa (now generally known as Taiwan) was even more mysterious than Japan, Psalmanazar was able to make up his own "Formosan" language. Anglican churchmen, impressed with Psalmanazar's piety and erudition, paid him to instruct missionaries in this unknown tongue. The church also commissioned him to translate the Bible into "Formosan!"

Much to his amazement and amusement, Psalmanazar was installed at Oxford to lecture on his "homeland." At this distinguished institution he schooled several students in the Formosan language.

In 1704, he even published a book entitled *An Historical and Geographical Description of Formosa*, which enjoyed much popular success. Psalmanazar provided juicy tidbits such as the "fact" that Formosans sacrificed 18,000 babies to their gods each New Year's Day, and that they ate raw meat. To make the latter point more graphically, Psalmanazar himself ate uncooked meat in public. To make Formosans seem a more palatable people, Psalmanazar declared that classical Greek was taught in all the island's colleges!

Psalmanazar's hilarious hoax ended in 1706, when increasing suspicions and accusations from abroad forced him to repudiate his assertions. He remained in England, doing all sorts of literary hack work to survive. His *Memoirs of (a man) Commonly Known by the Name George Psalmanazar* was published in 1764, the year after his death.

Claude Seurat was the skinniest man who ever lived

Claude Ambroise Seurat, better known as "The Living Skeleton," was born at Troyes, France on

April 10, 1797. His parents were poor but robust people, and their infant son seemed destined to follow in their footsteps—Claude was an apparently normal child of average size. But as he grew in stature, his weight did not increase correspondingly. Indeed, what little flesh he possessed as an infant seemed to wither away. At full maturity, Claude had a back-to-chest thickness of only *three inches*, one inch less than the measurement of his puny biceps.

In 1825, at the age of 28, Seurat agreed to exhibit himself in London. On the way northwest from his native Troyes, he stopped at Rouen, where no fewer than 1,500 people crowded around him in one day. A contemporary account of Seurat's London premiere on August 9, 1825, is given by a Mr. Hone in the *Every Day Book*. Hone was "instantly riveted by [Seurat's] amazing emaciation; he seemed another 'Lazarus come forth' without his grave-clothes...My eye, then, first caught the arm as the most remarkable limb; from the shoulder to the elbow it is like an ivory German flute...not having a trace of muscle, it is as perfect a cylinder as a writing rule."

Seurat's head was the only part of his body that was not shrunken. Accordingly, neither were his faculties in any way diminished. Seurat was smart enough to extract a small fortune from this London exhibition, though he did not live long enough to enjoy it.

The seven-year-old who died of old age

Charles Charlesworth first saw the light of day on March 14, 1829. No one in his home town of Straffordshire, England, had any reason to doubt that he would be anything but a happy and healthy child. And indeed, the boy's first years were blissfully ordinary.

At the age of four, however, little Charles sprouted whiskers and reached sexual maturity. Aging rapidly over the next three years, Charles developed conspicuous veins and tendons, white hair, shriveled skin, and the gait and posture of a man ten times his age.

One day in his seventh year, Charles fainted and did not revive. The remarkable child had expired of natural causes, the coroner ruled—merely old age.

Blondin crossed over Niagara Falls on a tightrope while pushing a wheelbarrow

Jean François Grandet, who performed under the name of Blondin because of his flowing blond hair, was the daredevil supreme. In 1859, he had a three-inch thick rope strung 1,100 feet across Niagara Falls, 160 feet above the raging waters. Balancing himself with a 40-foot pole, the intrepid Frenchman pedaled over the Falls on a bicycle.

Scorning death, he once walked over the tightrope blindfolded. On another day, he pushed a wheelbarrow across the Falls on the tightrope.

On one occasion, he announced he was going to carry a man across the chasm piggy-back style. One hundred thousand curious Americans and Canadians came to Niagara to see that one. The only person he could get to do the stunt with him was his manager, who trembled so violently that Blondin vowed never to do a stunt with a human again.

Always dreaming up new ways to astound the spectators, Blondin would turn somersaults on the rope. He would also have a man below the Falls shoot bullets through a hat he held up as a target. The acrobat even cooked and ate an egg prepared on a frying pan heated on a stove which he had carried out to the middle of the rope himself!

One of his most fantastic feats was to walk halfway out on the brightly lighted rope after dark and then order the light put out. When this was done, Blondin would continue to the other side in inky blackness.

On September 8, 1860, the Prince of Wales, who was touring North America, showed up in Canada to watch Blondin's final performance over the Falls. And what a show Blondin gave him!

Blondin attached short stilts to his legs; on each stilt, there was a hook which went around the rope. Halfway across the gorge, Blondin swung by the hooks head-down from the rope. Scores of men and women fainted, believing that he had lost his balance, fallen, and was going to plunge to his death. But Blondin had planned it all as a show-stopper. Hanging by the hooks, he swung gaily in his perilous position, and then nonchalantly got up and continued on to the Canadian shore.

Mihailo Tolotos never saw a woman

Mihailo Tolotos, a Greek monk who died in 1938 at the age of 82, was perhaps the only man never to have laid eyes on a woman. Mihailo's mother died when he was born, and the infant was whisked away the following day to a monastery atop Mount Athos. Tolotos spent the remainder of his life among the monks—completely isolated from female society. Women and *even female animals* were prohibited from entering the monastery, a tradition dating back to the founding of the retreat more than nine centuries earlier.

Mozart wrote a symphony when he was only eight years old

Mozart was the greatest musical genius the world has ever known. His accomplishments were so breathtaking that they are hardly believable; yet the amazing facts given here have all been authenticated.

Wolfgang Amadeus Mozart began playing the harpsichord when he was only three. He seemed to learn everything almost instinctively, and never had to be told twice about anything relating to music. In fact, his ear was so sensitive that it could detect an aberration of even an eighth of a note in the tuning of a violin string.

Wolfgang's father used to play in a string quartet. One day, the quartet was playing at the home of the senior Mozart. The second violinist had failed to come, and young Mozart, then five, took the missing musician's place. He had never seen the music before, but he played it as if he had been practicing it for weeks. His father and the other musicians expressed great amazement, but the child merely shrugged and said, "Surely you don't have to study and practice to play *second* violin, do you?"

Wolfgang started to compose music almost as early in life as he learned to play music. He wrote two minuets for the harpsichord when he was five years old. When he was seven, he wrote a creditable sonata; and, unbelievable as it seems, he was only eight when he wrote a complete symphony.

The elder Mozart knew he had a prodigy on his hands, and he took Wolfgang on a tour of the musical capitals of Europe. The young Mozart played with a mature understanding that electrified the great musicians of Europe. Moreover, the youngster performed feats that were near miracles—tricks of ear and memory that baffled everyone. A melody would be played just once; Mozart would listen and reproduce it faithfully without a flaw. Blindfolded, he would identify all the elements of a chord, no matter on what instrument it was played. He would be given intricate scores to read at sight, and would then play them with a precision that could be equaled only by a first-rate musician who had practiced for hours, or perhaps days.

In Rome, once a year during Holy Week, the *Miserere* of Gregorio Allegri was performed by the

papal choir. The Pope had forbidden its performance anywhere else in the world, and the only copy of the score in existence had been jealously guarded in the papal vaults. A decree issued by the Vatican prohibited anyone from reproducing this holy work in any form. Transgression was to be punished by excommunication.

The *Miserere* was a lengthy, complex contrapuntal composition. Mozart heard it played once. Returning to his room, he transcribed the entire score from memory! The Pope heard about this feat and was so moved by this manifestation of utter genius that instead of anathematizing the boy, he bestowed upon him the Cross of the Order of the Golden Spur.

Before he died in 1791, Wolfgang Amadeus Mozart had produced some 600 operas, operettas, concertos for piano and string quartet, sonatas for the violin, serenades, motets, masses, and many other types of classical music. Perhaps the most astounding fact about this prolific and brilliant production is that Mozart only lived to the age of 35.

"To keep from dying," Sarah Winchester built a 160-room house

Mrs. Sarah Winchester's mansion near San Jose, California, grew to be the world's largest private dwelling—all because of Mrs. Winchester's odd fear. She was sure she would die as soon as her house was finished.

Mrs. Winchester was heir to the $20 million "Winchester Rifle" fortune, and it has been suggested that her bizarre compulsion to build was the result of her uneasiness over the many deaths caused by her father's invention. Scores of carpenters, masons, and plumbers were kept busy every day for nearly 38 years in order to satisfy Sarah Winchester's mania.

Some rooms were built and furnished with all the elegance of an Oriental palace. Gold and silver chandeliers hung from the ceilings. Floors were inlaid with rare woods. Walls were covered with satin.

Other parts of the house were built just so that Mrs. Winchester could hear the bang of the hammers. Some rooms actually measured only a few inches wide, and some stairways led nowhere!

The crazy house contained 2,000 doors and 10,000 windows, many of which opened onto blank walls.

When Mrs. Winchester died in 1922 at the age of 83, her mansion had 160 rooms and sprawled over six acres. The house was seven stories high and boasted three elevators, three heating systems, 47 fireplaces, nine kitchens, and miles of secret passages and hallways. The total cost of all this insane labor was over $5,000,000.

The woman who would not talk

Here is a cautionary tale for henpecked husbands. After reading about Madame Regnier, you may have second thoughts about telling your wife to button her lip.

Madame Regnier lived comfortably in Versailles as the wife of a French Royal Procurator, or crown attorney. One fine day in 1842, she was prattling about something or other when her husband admonished her, "Be silent, woman, you talk nonsense."

Madame Regnier stormed out of the room in a huff. For days afterward, she would not speak to her husband—nor to anyone else. At last, Monsieur Regnier went to his wife's chamber and abjectly apologized. His wife looked at him impassively, and said not a word.

Days stretched into weeks, and weeks into years, while Madame Regnier continued to hold her tongue. Even when her daughter came to ask for permission to marry, Madame Regnier only nodded her assent.

From that day in 1842 to her death 30 years later, Madame Regnier never uttered a sound.

Benjamin Franklin, the most versatile American

Benjamin Franklin said, "I wish the good Lord had seen fit to make the day twice as long as it is.

Perhaps then I could *really* accomplish something."

Thus spoke this many-sided man who did any number of things—and did them all amazingly well. He was a painter, writer, publisher, scientist, statesman, inventor, businessman, philosopher, and humanitarian.

Franklin's father, a poor Boston candlemaker, hoped to make Benjamin, one of 17 children, a minister. But lack of funds forced young Franklin to leave school at the age of 10. Apprenticed to an older brother, a printer, Benjamin managed to educate himself by giving up meat and using the money saved to buy books. Young Benjamin not only educated himself in such basic subjects as arithmetic and English grammar, but also in navigation, algebra, geometry, and philosophy.

In 1723, at the age of 17, Ben left Boston to try his luck in Philadelphia. He arrived in that colonial town with little money and no friends. Yet within a very few years, Franklin became a famous author and publisher. His sharp wit and common-sense advice, published in his *Pennsylvania Gazette* and *Poor Richard's Almanack*, were known throughout the American colonies.

Marked up to his credit are a series of diverse achievements never equaled in American history.

Here are just a few of his accomplishments:

As a scientist and inventor, Franklin:

1. Proved that lightning consisted of electricity.

2. Invented the lightning rod.

3. Invented the Franklin stove, an economical and useful heating device.

4. Invented bifocal glasses.

5. Invented the platform rocking chair.

6. Wrote a scientific essay which for the first time described the existence of the Gulf Stream.

7. Discovered that poorly aired rooms spread disease.

In the realm of literature, Franklin:

1. Was an original and highly talented writer, whose *Poor Richard's Almanack* and *Autobiography* have assumed a permanent place in the American literary heritage.

2. Founded a popular publication, the *Pennsylvania Gazette*, later to become *The Saturday Evening Post*.

As a humanitarian and tireless contributor to the public welfare, Franklin:

1. Organized the first fire department in Philadelphia.

2. Helped establish the first hospital in America.

3. Founded the first lending library in America.

4. Created the first efficient postal system in America.

5. Founded an academy which later became the University of Pennsylvania.

6. Headed the first society in America to oppose slavery.

7. Established the first American fire insurance company.

8. Founded a club that later became the American Philosophical Society.

Though his accomplishemtns in any of these fields would have assured Franklin a lasting imprint on American history, it was his role in founding a new nation that gave Franklin his special place in the hearts of his countrymen.

Although he had already attained the advanced age of 70 when the Revolutionary War broke out in 1776, Franklin's guiding hand was felt everywhere during the struggle against the British. As Postmaster General of the colonies in rebellion, he contributed his entire salary to help the American wounded. Franklin also took a major part in reorganizing the Continental Army into an efficient fighting force. He helped draft the Declaration of Independence and, as America's envoy to France, did much to forge the alliance that in 1778 brought French aid to the hard-pressed American troops. And it was Franklin's wisdom and gift for compromise that, once the Revolution was won, helped the colonies become a united nation under a federal constitution.

A year before Franklin's death, George Washington wrote the following words to this universally admired American. "If to be venerated for benevolence, if to be admired for talent, if to be esteemed for patriotism, if to be beloved for philanthropy, can gratify the human mind, you must have the pleasing consolation to know you have not lived in vain."

Theogenes fought and killed 1,425 opponents

In ancient days, the rulers of Greece and Rome would amuse themselves and their subjects

through gladiatorial combats in which men fought to the death for the amusement of the spectators. History records that the greatest of these gladiators was a Greek called Theogenes, a native of Thasos.

Theogenes served a cruel prince named Thesus, who reigned about 900 B.C. Thesus delighted in sadistic spectacles and ordained a combat that was especially vicious. The two contestants—if they can be called such—were placed facing each other, almost nose to nose, each on a flat stone. Both men were strapped into place. Their fists were encased in leather thongs which were studded with small, sharp metal spikes. At a given signal, they would strike at each other, and the combat would continue, without rest, until one of the contestants had been beaten to death.

During a long career, Theogenes—strong, skillful and savage—faced 1,425 men and killed every one of them.

Javier Pereira lived to be 169

In 1956, a Colombian Indian named Javier Pereira was brought to the Cornell Medical Center of New York Hospital to undergo a battery of tests to determine his age. Pereira had caused quite a stir with his claim that he had been born in 1789—the year of George Washington's inauguration as President. Author Doug Storer had discovered this ancient Indian, and Storer determined to show Pereira to the world.

The doctors at New York Hospital could make no exact determination of Pereira's age, but they went on record as saying that he was certainly "over 150 years old."

Shortly after Pereira died in April, 1958, at the age of 169, the Colombian government issued a postage stamp commemorating this modern Methuselah.

Giuseppe de Mai had two hearts in his body

When anything pleased Giuseppe de Mai, a resident of Naples, he was doubly excited, for not one, but two, hearts pounded away inside his chest.

This condition occurs so rarely that scientists throughout Europe became interested in Signor de Mai. In 1894, the London Academy of Medicine offered de Mai $15,000 to obtain his body after Giuseppe died.

King Otto of the hundred hours

In 1913, Albanian revolutionaries threw off the yoke of the Ottoman Empire and established their nation as an independent state. For a nominal ruler, the little Moslem nation on the Adriatic naturally looked to Turkey, and chose Prince Helim Eddine.

The capital city of Durazzo was decorated colorfully and the people crowded together to welcome the prince's carriage. The first to emerge was a seven-foot man in an ornate military costume, with a saber at his side and a fez atop his head. "Stand back," he cried. "Make way for the new Prince of Albania!" The second man out of the carriage was not so tall, but exceedingly broad in the chest and shoulders.

After these two, the Prince stepped forward, to the cheers of the masses. After a few words of greeting, Helim Eddine offered his first official decree: that he was now a citizen of Albania, not Turkey, and that there would be a week of general celebration and an amnesty for all prisoners. The people responded wildly to this magnanimous gesture. The new nation had a new national hero.

That night, at a feast, Helim Eddine was presented with a 25-woman harem. As befit a Moslem ruler, he gratefully accepted this gift. The next day, he further endeared himself to the natives of Durazzo by appointing the city's councilmen to be his cabinet. The councilmen were so honored that they moved to promote the Prince to King. The Prince graciously acceded to their wishes, suggesting that as King he be known as King Otto. This puzzled the cabinet members, since Otto was a distinctly non-Moslem name. Nevertheless, they had no reason to stand in his way.

It was not until the fifth day of King Otto's reign that the general gaiety waned. A wire arrived in the prime minister's office. It was signed by the real Eddine who was still in Turkey, and who was quite puzzled by reports that he had arrived in Durazzo.

The picture started to become clear. The prime minister rushed to the imperial chambers, but

"King Otto" and his two aides-de-camp were gone.

A long investigation into the matter revealed that King Otto was, in fact, one Otto Witte, a circus performer. His two aides had been the circus giant and the circus strong man.

Albania had lost a king, but Otto Witte had enjoyed the best four days of his life.

O'Higgins won a battle with an army of animals

In 1814, Bernardo O'Higgins headed a small army of Chilean patriots who had been trying to free their country from Spanish rule since 1810. Though they had few arms, the Chileans often managed to give the Spaniards a bad time.

The Spanish king sent boatloads of soldiers to wipe out O'Higgins and his patriot army. But the Chileans fought with such courage and skill that, weak and outnumbered though they were, they could not be vanquished. Nevertheless, under this constant onslaught, O'Higgins' ragged men were being forced to retreat, day by day. It seemed only a matter of time until their backs would be up against a wall.

Just outside the Chilean city of Santiago lay the small town of Rancagua. Here, on October 1 and 2, O'Higgins and his army made a desperate stand. Worn out by days of fighting, tortured by thirst and merciless heat, the Chileans stood surrounded.

Then came a terrible blow. O'Higgins himself was struck by an enemy bullet.

The Chilean patriots seemed doomed to defeat, when the wounded O'Higgins conceived a plan.

He ordered his men to round up as many mules, cows, sheep, and dogs as possible. Barns, stables, and pastures were emptied of their livestock, and all the animals were quickly mustered before the commander.

With the vast herd of animals assembled before him, O'Higgins was lifted to his horse. Then, with

a shout and a lash of his whip, O'Higgins sent his steed charging ahead. The frightened animals began to run. Soon they became a stampeding, bellowing mass. O'Higgins drove them on and on—straight for the Spanish lines. Maddened by fear, the animals paid little heed to the formidable array of soldiers before them.

The Spanish veterans had never seen such a thundering horde. Terrified, they broke ranks and ran!

Close on the heels of the charging beasts came O'Higgins and his men. They galloped through the path which the animals had made for them. Slashing with their swords, they sped through the Spanish lines.

Helpless and stunned, the Spaniards watched the Chileans escape. Before the Spaniards could reorganize their forces for pursuit, the Chileans were safe in the mountains. There they recuperated, enlisted new recruits, and gathered arms.

Three years alter, at the head of an army of 4,000 men, Bernardo O'Higgins returned to destroy the Spanish battalions. In 1818, O'Higgins proudly proclaimed Chile's independence from Spain, and became the first ruler of the new nation.

The king who shot a peasant a day

Here's the life of another King Otto, this one a real king from Bavaria. Otto gained the crown in 1886, but he was hardly fit to rule his subjects. For the previous 14 years, his raving lunacy had forced his family to keep him in a locked room. This constraint did not seem to bother Otto too much, because it did allow him the privacy necessary for his conferences with the spirits who lived in his dresser drawers.

One of Otto's more peculiar notions was that if he shot a peasant a day, he could keep the doctor away. The Mad King was enabled to gratify his whim by the compliance of two loyal guards. One guard would daily load Otto's gun with blanks, while the other would don peasant garb and hide in the bushes outside the King's window. When Otto would appear at the window with pistol poised, the "peasant" would emerge from his hiding place and amiably drop dead at the sound of the shot.

Robert Wadlow was 8 feet 11 inches tall

When Robert Wadlow was born in 1918 in Alton, Illinois, no one paid special attention to his arrival except his parents and relatives. For Robert was an ordinary baby, tipping the scales at a healthy eight-and-a-half pounds.

But young Robert began to grow and grow. At the age of five, he was 5′4″; at 10 he was 6′5″; at 14, 7′5″; at 18, he soared by three inches—and he still kept growing! This spectacular growth caused Robert to have difficulty with one foot, on which he had to wear a heavy metal brace.

Eventually, the brace led to an infection of the ankle. The fever caused by the infection claimed Wadlow's life in Manistee, Michigan, at the age of 22. At his death, Robert Wadlow was the tallest man in recorded medical history, at a fraction more than 8′11″.

John Gully boxed his way from prison to Parliament

One day in 1805, Henry Pierce, heavyweight boxing champion of England, came to a debtors' prison to entertain the inmates. For Pierce's

victim, the warden chose John Gully. To the warden's surprise, and the howling cheers of his fellow convicts, Gully battered Pierce all around the ring.

The taverns soon were bubbling with the story of Gully's victory. A group of gamblers determined to pay off Gully's debts, and get him out of prison. To repay the gamblers, Gully agreed to fight exhibition bouts for them.

And Gully really fought. He fought so well that he soon amassed sufficient winnings to buy himself out of the clutches of the gamblers.

From 1806 on, Gully managed himself. He signed for an official championship bout with Henry Pierce, and lost the fight in the 59th round. But after that single defeat, he never was beaten again. When Pierce retired in 1807, John Gully was acclaimed heavyweight champion of England.

Unlike many prize fighters, Gully saved his money and knew when it was time to quit. He left the boxing ring, and invested his savings in horse racing. Two of his horses won the famous English Derby.

And then John Gully took a real jump—all the way from the race track to politics. In 1832, he was elected to the House of Commons. Thereafter, he served several terms in Parliament.

When he died in 1863 at the great age of 90, Gully left a substantial fortune and a fine country estate.

And it all began with a roundhouse right...

The countess who operated on herself

In the mid-19th century, the wealthiest noble in Poland was the Countess Rosa Branicka. Her assets were valued at some 20 million dollars and her lands were worked by 125,000 serfs.

In 1843, the health of the 63-year-old Countess began to fail, and she went to Germany to receive expert diagnosis of her ailment. There she learned that she was suffering from cancer of the breast. The doctors recommended immediate surgery.

But the Countess, perhaps not willing to frighten her family, would not agree to an operation. Instead, she traveled through Germany, Switzerland, and France, buying various surgical instruments in various towns. She would buy a scalpel in one place, a lancet in the other— but never more than one item in any one place, so that no one might guess her intentions.

When she had finally assembled all the instruments that she thought were necessary, Countess Branicka secluded herself in a Paris hotel. There she removed the cancer from her breast. Her recuperation was swift, and she soon returned to Poland where she lived to the ripe age of 82.

Azzar lay on a bed of nails for 25½ hours

The fakirs of the mysterious East claim to have performed fantastic feats of endurance. But many fakirs are no more than common fakers, and upon

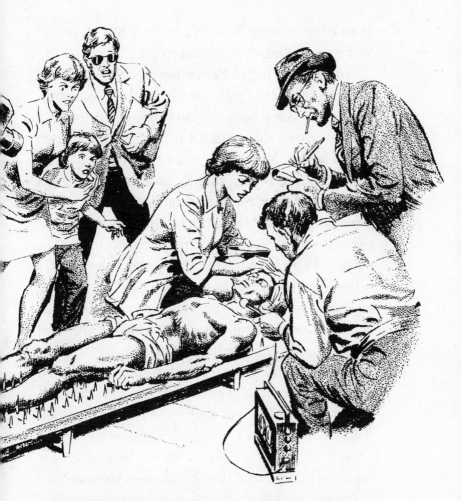

investigation it usually turns out that their purported feats took place under circumstances that tender their claims dubious.

In Sydney, Australia, there is a fakir who backed up his claims by performing in the presence of newsmen and numerous other spectators, outside Walton's on Park Street, one of Sydney's leading department stores.

On the morning of November 20, 1969, bearded Zjane Azzar, clad only in turban and loincloth, gingerly lowered himself into a prone position on a bed of razor-sharp six-inch nails, spaced two inches apart from each other. Throughout that day, the following night, and into the next morning, Azzar remained on his bed of nails, refreshing himself from time to time by smoking a cigarette or by eating a hamburger and some ice cream. During much of this period, he clearly suffered considerable pain. Once his pulse reading was so weak that the attending nurse had to use hot and cold compresses to revive him, and wanted to call the whole thing off.

Azzar refused. He remained stretched out on his bed of nails for a total of twenty-five-and-one-half hours, surpassing all such previously recorded feats. As Azzar tried to raise himself at the end of his ordeal, he said, "My body has been dead for fourteen hours," and then he fainted. He was later examined by a doctor who found him weak, but despite the pattern of deep indentations in his back, the fakir was little damaged physically.

Chang and Eng, the original Siamese twins

"Siamese twins" are two separate, identical organisms, each a complete or nearly complete individual. While such births occur with some frequency, only rarely do the twins survive.

Siamese twins may be joined at either the chest, the abdomen, the back, or the top of the head. In cases where the twins share a vital organ, surgical division is not possible, and the twins must go through life together, just as Chang and Eng did in the last century.

Chang and Eng were born in 1811 of Chinese parents in Siam (whence the name for the condition). They were joined at the breastbone, but were otherwise fully developed, independent beings. They toured with P.T. Barnum's circus for years before settling down as farmers in North Carolina. They adopted the last name of Bunker—why, no one knows—and simultaneously married the daughters of a farmer named Yates.

Chang and Eng each ran his own farm one mile from the other's. How, you ask? Chang and Eng would spend three days of each week with one wife and three days with the other wife. What they did on the seventh day, the Lord only knows.

They lived very happily in North Carolina, and between them produced 22 offspring. When one twin died on January 17, 1874, the other survived for only two more hours.

Johnny Eck walked on his hands

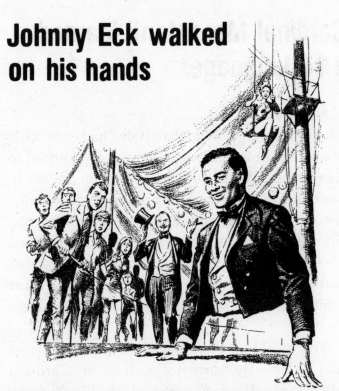

Johnny Eck did not walk on his hands as a stunt; that was the only way he could get around, for he was born without a body below the waist. Johnny's arms were longer than his body, and so powerful that he could stand on one hand easily. He did have two feet, but they were malformed and useless.

Eck made his living in the circus, where he was bluntly called The Half Man. But Johnny lived a whole life; he was an excellent pianist and saxophonist who for a time had his own orchestra.

Cardinal Mezzofanti learned 114 languages

Joseph Caspar of Bologna, Italy, had very little schooling. At an early age, he was apprenticed to a carpenter. While working in the shop one day in the mid-1780's, he heard a priest next door giving lessons in Greek and Latin to some students. Though he was not even in the class, and had never seen a book in either language, the young carpenter proved to be the best pupil. In a short while, he was able to speak both languages fluently.

The would-be carpenter later became a priest and eventually earned the title of Cardinal Mezzofanti. He spent most of his life studying languages, learning to speak at least 53 languages with considerable fluency. He spoke 61 additional tongues not quite so well, and understood 72 more dialects, although he could not speak them.

The only language to provide Cardinal Mezzofanti any difficulty at all was Chinese, which took the master linguist all of four months to learn!

How much does one have to travel to learn languages? Cardinal Mezzofanti never once left Italy in his whole life!

Wickham plunged into the sea from a height of 205 feet

"I'll dive anywhere!" Alex Wickham was fond of saying. "You supply the board and the water, and I'll do the jumping!"

And jump he did, even when his friends set the board atop a cliff overlooking the Yarra River near

Melbourne, Australia. On March 22, 1918, Wickham climbed onto the diving board and plunged off in perfect diving form. Halfway down, he lost consciousness, and he hit the water with such force that his bathing suit was ripped

from his body. Fortunately, he regained consciousness upon impact.

After Wickham came to the surface and swam to shore, his stunned admirers measured the height of the cliff. It was 205 feet 9 inches high. Wickham had leaped from a perch as high as a 15-story building—and lived!